Editor
Kim Fields

Managing Editors
Karen J. Goldfluss, M.S. Ed.
Ina Massler Levin, M.A.

Editorial Project Manager
Mara Ellen Guckian

Illustrator
Kelly McMahon

Cover Artist
Barb Lorseyedi

Art Manager
Kevin Barnes

Art Director
CJae Froshay

Imaging
Craig Gunnell
Rosa C. See

Publisher
Mary D. Smith, M.S. Ed.

A Poem In My Pocket
Winter

Grades Pre-K–1

muffin · puffin

Winter Weather
by _____

tall

Author

Traci Ferguson Geiser, M.A.

Teacher Created Resources

Teacher Created Resources, Inc.
6421 Industry Way
Westminster, CA 92683
www.teachercreated.com
ISBN-1-4206-3141-1

Table of Contents

Introduction

A *Poem in My Pocket: Winter* was designed to provide busy teachers with hassle-free, developmentally appropriate literacy experiences for young children. All of the activities included in each unit will help children develop prereading skills and give them fun, hands-on experiences with print. Phonological awareness skills such as rhyming, syllabication, and beginning and ending sounds are the focus of each lesson. Students will review lines of poetry, observing sentences and punctuation. Further, they will have opportunities to point out the words forming each sentence and note the syllables (and phonemes) used to make different words.

The *Poem in My Pocket* series consists of three seasonally themed books: *Fall*, *Winter*, and *Spring*. The books include five units, each containing a full week of thematic lesson plans based on an original poem. The *Winter* book incorporates the following themes: Winter Weather, Arctic Animals, Animals in Winter, Planets, and Dinosaurs.

Each unit includes the following components:

Original Poem: Each poem in the book was created to enhance the topics typically explored in preschool and kindergarten. Each poem can be enlarged to display in the classroom or copied to create a book of poetry for your classroom library. These simple poems will complement existing curriculum and help build oral language skills. Reproducible Pocket Chart Cards and Picture Cards are included for each poem and require minimal teacher preparation.

Daily Interactive Pocket Chart Activities: Using the poem text, students will participate in hands-on games and activities that will promote prereading skills, including phonological awareness. Lesson plans for each day focus on essential emergent literacy skills, including letter and sound recognition, rhyming, syllabication, basic sight words, and basic punctuation. The week's activities culminate with a fun Home/School Connection activity.

Home/School Connection: The week's activities culminate with a fun Home/School Connection activity. A letter pertaining to the weekly theme is included to copy and send home to parents and caregivers. This letter invites parents to take an active role in their children's learning by assisting in a prereading activity, thus fostering literacy development. This letter will encourage parent involvement and extend learning into the home.

Student Poem Page: A page containing the unit's poem, with ample room for children's illustrations, is included. Use this page to help develop fine motor skills, left-to-right correspondence, and oral language.

Mini Book: The Mini Book for each poem will allow children interactive practice with books and book parts such as reading from front-to-back, left-to-right, and top-to-bottom. The end of each Mini Book contains a simple activity that will offer children an opportunity to interact with the poem's text.

Literature Links: A list of related children's literature is included to complement the unit, and help generate and retain interest in the unit's theme.

How to Use This Book

Before you begin teaching the lessons, you will need to gather some supplies. A basic pocket chart with ten pockets will be needed to hold the Pocket Chart Cards. Pocket charts are available at most teacher supply stores and will be an asset to your early childhood classroom by giving your students additional opportunities to interact with print. You may also wish to invest in a pocket chart stand to provide quick, roll-away storage for your pocket chart. You will need a few basic office supplies to prepare and complete each lesson, including scissors, crayons, a stapler, tape, and markers.

Prior to starting each unit, you will need to prepare each of the following:

1. Reproduce the Home/School Connection Letter for each student. Go over the activity with your class before sending it home to be sure they understand what they are being asked to do with their parents. You may want to offer a special reward (sticker or small toy) for children who complete the activity.

2. Cut out the Pocket Chart Cards and Picture Cards for the unit. You may want to laminate the cards or attach them to tagboard for durability since all of the activities are hands-on and the cards will be handled a great deal. You can color the Picture Cards if you wish, just be certain to read the entire unit first to determine if there are any special color requirements for the pictures. Arranging the cards in the correct order and storing them in a large envelope or resealable plastic bag will help with organization and management of each poem. Commercial sentence strip file boxes can also be purchased at your local teacher supply store.

3. Reproduce and assemble a poem Mini Book for each student. Copy the pages, cut them out, and put them in order. Staple the pages on the left-hand side to create a small book version of the poem for each child to take home. Encourage the children to read their books to their families and friends at home.

4. Reproduce the Student Poem Page for each child. After the child has illustrated the page, hold on to it. Once several units are complete, you may want to compile these individual pages into a booklet for each child to take home periodically and read to their families. Using an inexpensive folder for three-hole-punched paper will allow you to add additional poems to the booklets as you complete them.

   Make a mini pointer for the poem collection folder. Attach a 12" string or piece of yarn to one end of a craft stick. Tie the other end of the string or yarn to a ring in the folder. Children can use the pointer to point to the words as they read each poem.

   At the end of the year, give each child a large sheet of folded construction paper to decorate and use as a cover. Staple the poems inside. Save the original mini-binders to use again next year.

5. You may wish to find the Literature Links or other books on the theme in your school or neighborhood library. Reading these books will help generate interest and extend the knowledge the children gain from the unit. Keep the books in an accessible place in the reading area once they have been introduced.

   Optional: Each unit begins with a full-page copy of the poem. These pages can be enlarged, colored, and displayed in the classroom. Another option is to copy the pages and create a book for the class library once all the poems have been shared.

Winter Weather

Flakes fall,

Breezes blow,

We play in

Slushy snow.

Wind wails,

Branches bare,

We stay warm in

Winter wear.

Winter Weather

Unit Preparation

Copy and send home the Winter Weather Home/School Connection Parent Letter and Homework Page (pages 8–9). Copy and cut apart the Winter Weather Pocket Chart Cards (pages 10–13). Copy, color, and cut out the Winter Weather Picture Cards (pages 14–15). Place all the cards in the pocket chart in the correct places. Copy, color, and cut out the Winter Weather Clothing Cards (pages 22–23) and Winter Weather /ch/ and /sh/ Picture Cards (pages 24–25). Copy the Winter Weather Student Poem Page (page 16) and *Winter Weather* Mini Book pages (17–21) for each child. See page 4 for additional preparation tips.

Student Poem Page

Ask the children to think about activities they like to do during the winter. Have them think about the types of clothes that are necessary to participate in those winter activities. Make a list of winter wear on the board or a chart. Assist each student in filling in the blank at the bottom of the Student Poem Page with his or her favorite winter activity. Have each child draw a picture to illustrate the sentence, making sure to include the appropriate winter wear as part of the picture.

Mini Book

Assemble the *Winter Weather* Mini Book pages (17–21) for each child. Have the children color the pages and read their mini books to others. At the end of the week, invite each child to take the book home and read it to his or her family.

Literature Links

The Biggest, Best Snowman by Margery Cuyler (Scholastic, 2004)

The Biggest Snowball Ever! by John Rogan (Turtleback Books, 1998)

Katy and the Big Snow by Virginia Lee Burton (Houghton Mifflin, 1974)

The Snowy Day by Ezra Jack Keats (Viking Books, 1996)

Thomas' Snowsuit by Robert Munsch (Annick Press, 1985)

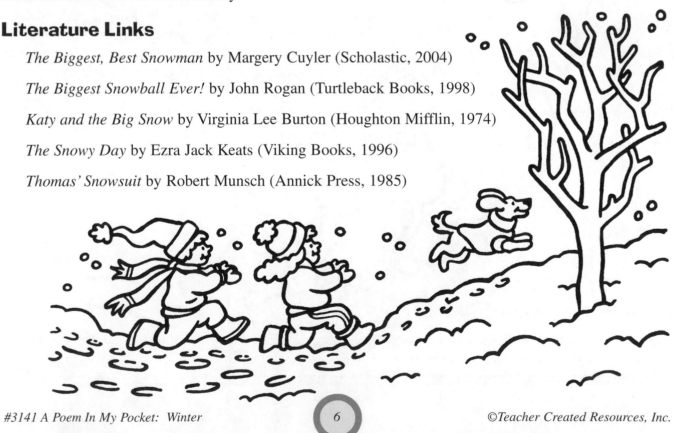

Pocket Chart Activities

Monday: Introduce the Poem

Read the poem, "Winter Weather," aloud to the children. Reread the poem, pointing to the words as you go. Look at the last line in the poem and ask the children what they think winter wear is. Hold up each of the Clothing Cards (pages 22–23) and ask the children if they think each item would be good to wear in the winter and why.

Tuesday: Same Sounds

Read the poem together as a class. Reread the poem, stopping to look for words that begin with the same sound in each line. Go around the circle and ask each child to say his or her name aloud. Have the child say the sound that is at the beginning of his or her name. Ask if any other students have the same sound at the beginning of their names. Have the students whose names begin with the same sound sit together. Continue until all of the children have determined the beginning sounds of their names.

Wednesday: /ch/ and /sh/

Place the /ch/ and /sh/ Picture Cards (pages 24–25) in a stack in front of you. Hold up the /ch/ card for the children and ask them to identify the picture. Tell them that the letters **ch** make the sound /ch/ when they are together, as in *chain*. Hold up the /sh/ card and ask the children to identify the picture. Tell them that the letters **sh** make the sound /sh/ when they are together, as in *shirt*. Read the poem together and ask the children to look (listen) for words containing /ch/ and /sh/ as they read (*slushy* and *branches*). Remove the cards from the pocket chart and place the /ch/ and /sh/ cards in the top pocket. Ask for two volunteers to put the words *branches* and *slushy* under the correct card according to the sound and letters found in it. Spread out the /ch/ and /sh/ Picture Cards on the floor. Ask a volunteer to choose a card, tell the class what it is, and then place it in the pocket chart under the correct card, according to which sound he or she hears in it. Continue until all the cards have been placed in the pocket chart. (Place the poem back in the pocket chart after completing this activity.)

Thursday: Phoneme Blending

In Phoneme Blending, children combine a series of phonemes to form a word. For example,

   Teacher: What is this word: /d/ /o/ /g/?

   Students: /d/ /o/ /g/ is *dog*

Practice phoneme blending using the following words from the poem: *fall, blow, play, snow, wind, bare, stay.* Point to each word in the poem after the children have successfully identified it.

Friday: Culminating Activity

Invite the children to bring their Homework Pages to circle time. Ask each child to read the pair of words he or she wrote in each set of mittens. Have the class verify that each set of words begins with the same sound. Reread the poem together one more time.

Winter Weather

Flakes fall,
Breezes blow,
We play in
Slushy snow.

Wind wails,
Branches bare,
We stay warm in
Winter wear.

Hello,

This week we will be learning this poem about winter weather. Please read the poem with your child to help him or her learn it. Using the poem as a springboard, we will work with beginning sounds in words, blend sounds together to form words (phoneme blending), and learn the sounds of /ch/ and /sh/.

Please help your child think of winter words that begin with the same sound. You might want to brainstorm a list of winter weather, clothing, and activities. Then, determine which words begin with the same sounds. On the attached Homework Page, help your child identify two pairs of words that begin with the same sound, for example *snow* and *scarf*. Have your child draw a picture and write the words for each pair of words inside a pair of mittens. If he or she is unable to write the words, you may assist your child or write them for him or her. Have your child bring the completed homework to school on

_____ .

Your child will be bringing home a *Winter Weather* Mini Book of the poem this week. Please ask him or her to read it to you. He or she may also want to read it to a special friend or relative.

Thank you for your sensational support!

Sincerely,

_____

Homework Page

Directions: Find two winter words that begin with the same sound. Write the words inside a pair of mittens. If your child is unable to write the words, assist your child or write it for him or her. Draw a picture for each word. Do the same thing for the second pair of mittens.

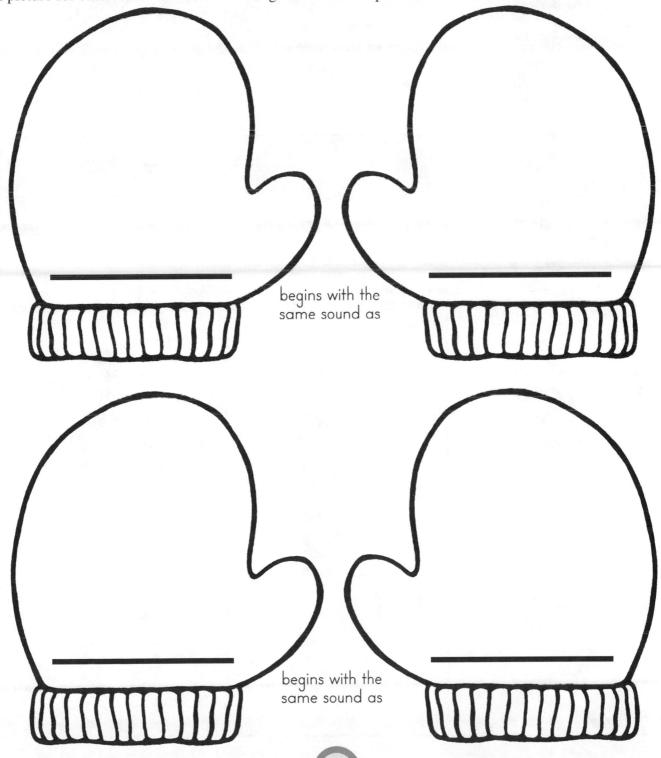

begins with the same sound as

begins with the same sound as

Winter Weather

fall,

blow,

Flakes

Breezes

play

Slushy

Wind

We

in

snow.

Branches

bare,

stay

wails,

We

in

wear.

warm

Winter

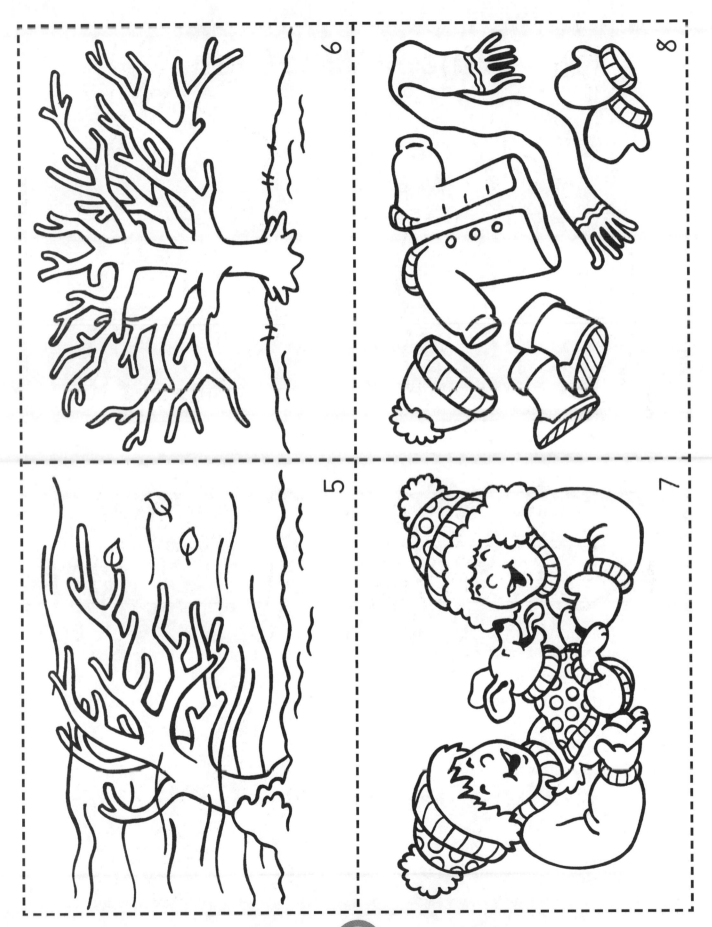

Winter Weather

Flakes fall,
Breezes blow,
We play in
Slushy snow.

Wind wails,
Branches bare,
We stay warm in
Winter wear.

I like to _____ in the winter.

Flakes fall,

1

Breezes blow,

We play in

Slushy snow.   4

Wind wails,   5

Branches bare,

We stay warm in

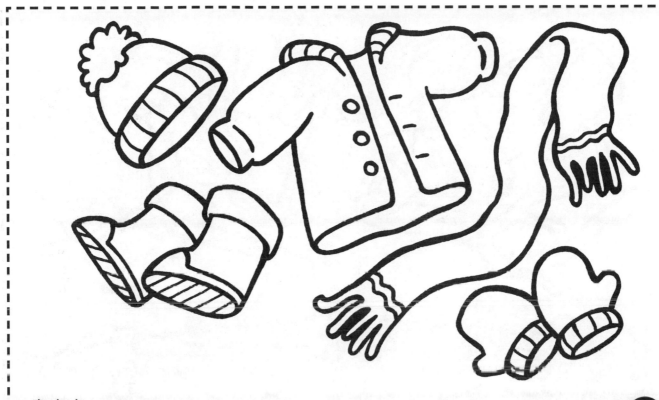

Winter wear. **8**

cozy

coat

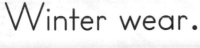

Use a red crayon to circle the words that begin with the same sound on each page. **9**

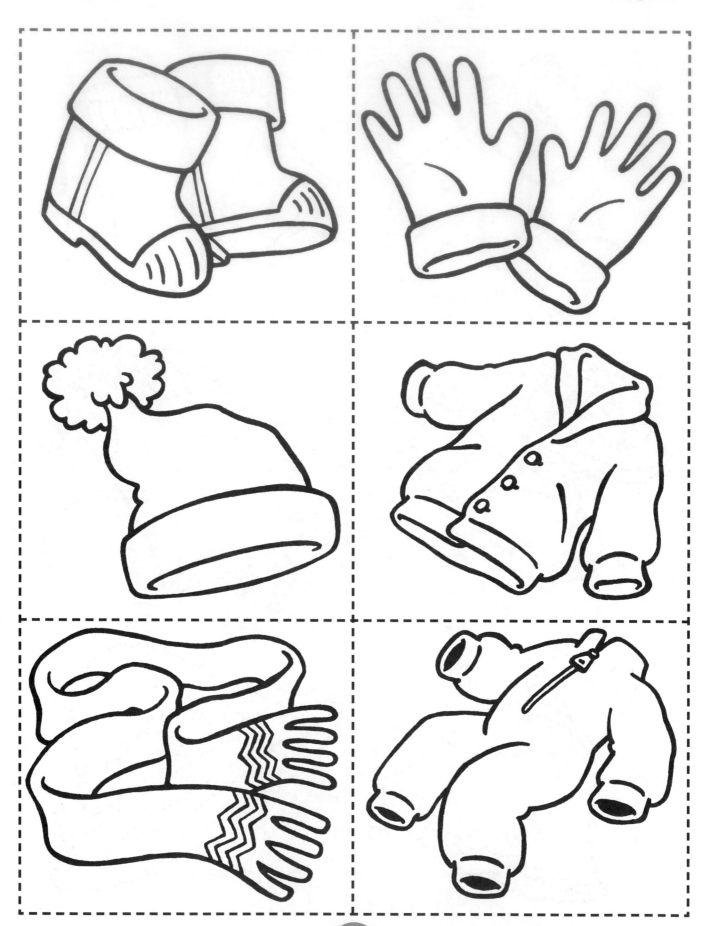

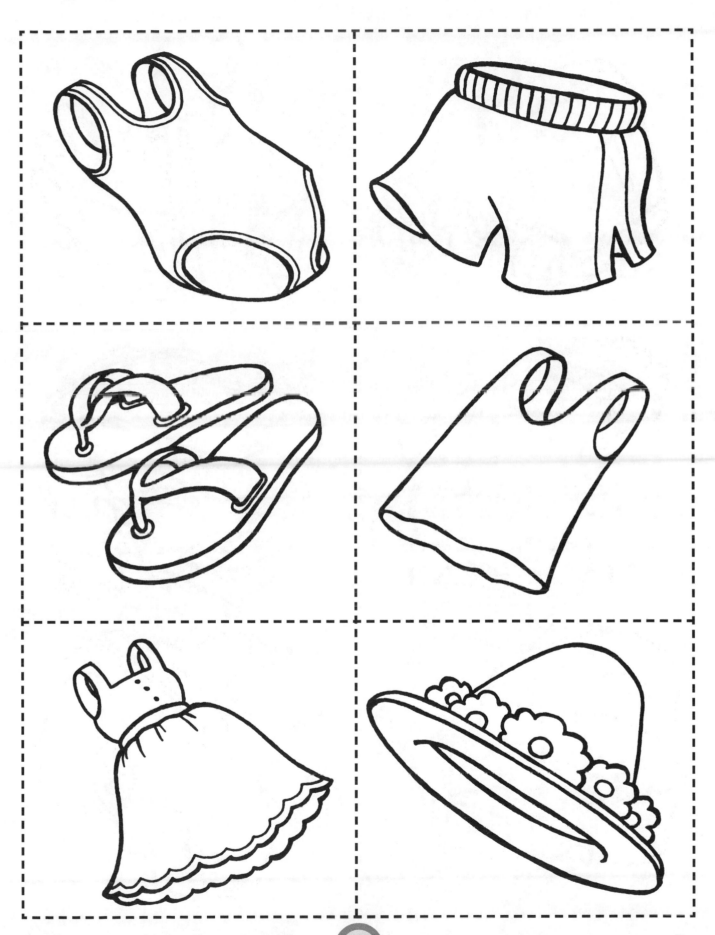

sh

Imagine . . .

Arctic Hare Jan
getting a tan.

Lemming Nell
ringing her bell.

Kip Caribou
sitting in an igloo.

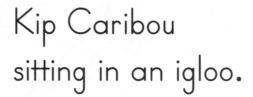

Freddy the Fox
wearing warm socks.

Pete Puffin
eating a muffin.

Unit Preparation

Arctic Animals

Copy, cut apart, and assemble a Homework Book (pages 30–32) for each child. Copy and send home the Arctic Animals Home/School Connection Parent Letter (page 29) along with the prepared Homework Book. Copy and cut apart the Arctic Animals *Imagine . . .* Pocket Chart Cards (pages 33–37). Copy, color, and cut out the Arctic Animals Picture Cards (pages 38–40). Place all the cards in the pocket chart in the correct places. Copy, color, and cut out the Arctic Animals Short Vowel Cards (page 48). Copy the Arctic Animals Imagine . . . Student Poem Page (page 41) and *Imagine . . .* Mini Book pages (pages 42–47) for each child. See page 4 for additional preparation tips.

Student Poem Page

Discuss arctic animals with the children. With the children's input, make a list of different arctic animals on the board or a chart. Ask the children to decide which arctic animal they like the best in the poem. Assist each child in locating the name in the text of the poem and writing it on the blank at the bottom of the Student Poem Page. Ask each child to illustrate his or her favorite animal performing the action indicated in the poem in the space provided.

Mini Book

Assemble an *Imagine . . .* Mini Book (pages 42–47) for each child. Have the children color the pages and read their Mini Books to others. At the end of the week, invite each child to take the book home and read it to his or her family.

Literature Links

Arctic Fives Arrive by Elinor J. Pinczes (Houghton Mifflin, 1996)

Far North in the Arctic: Counting Alaska's Animals by Cory Cooper Hansen (Sasquatch Books, 2004)

Hello, Arctic! by Theodore Taylor (Harcourt Children's Books, 2002)

Here Is Arctic Winter by Madeleine Dunphy (Hyperion, 1993)

Little Polar Bear, Take Me Home! by Hans de Beer (Nord-Sud Verlag, 2001)

Pocket Chart Activities

Monday: Introduce the Poem

Read the poem, "Imagine . . . " aloud to the children. Reread the poem, pointing to the words as you go. Invite the children to read the poem aloud with you. Ask the children if they know where the Arctic is. Using a globe or map, show the children where Arctic animals live.

Tuesday: Shorty and Friends

Read the poem with the class. Introduce short vowel sounds using the Short Vowel Cards (page 48). After the children are familiar with each of the short vowel sounds, ask them to reread the poem with you, looking for short vowel sounds in each line. After all of the short vowel sounds have been identified, ask a volunteer to come up and remove all of the words containing the short /a/ sound in the first two lines of the poem. Next, have another volunteer remove each word containing a short /e/ sound in the third and fourth lines of the poem. Continue in this manner until all of the short vowel sound words have been removed. Collect all of the cards and distribute them to the remaining students. Read the poem together, stopping where each missing card belongs and have the child that has the card replace it in the poem. Reread the poem one more time.

Wednesday: Phoneme Categorization

In Phoneme Categorization, children identify a word in a set of words that has a different sound. For example,

> **Teacher:** Which word doesn't belong in this set: *dog, hat, dad?*

> **Students:** *Dog* doesn't belong; it does not have the short /a/ sound.

Read the following sets of words from the poem (J**a**n, P**e**te, t**a**n; N**e**ll, b**e**ll, w**a**rm; **a**n, **i**n, K**i**p; s**o**cks, N**e**ll, f**o**x; p**u**ffin, m**u**ffin, Fr**e**ddy). Help your students practice phoneme categorization and short vowel sounds by having the class identify the word that doesn't belong according to its short vowel sound. After the children have determined which word in each set doesn't belong, read each set of words again and ask a student to find each word in the poem to verify that the matching words contain the same vowel letter. When you are finished, reread the poem together.

Thursday: -ing Endings

Write the letters *-ing* on the board or chart paper. Tell the class that these letters together are often found at the end of words. Have a volunteer find a word in the poem that ends with *-ing* and read it to the class. Continue until all six words ending in *-ing* (*getting, Lemming, ringing, sitting, wearing, eating*) have been found. Reread the poem together as a group.

Friday: Culminating Activity

Invite the children to bring their Homework Mini Books to the circle. Have each child choose one word he or she drew in the book and share which vowel sound it contains. Ask the class to determine if the correct vowel sound was identified. After all of the students have had a chance to share, reread the poem together one final time.

Imagine . . .

Arctic Hare Jan
getting a tan.
Lemming Nell
ringing her bell.
Kip Caribou
sitting in an igloo.
Freddy the Fox
wearing warm socks.
Pete Puffin
eating a muffin.

Hello,

This week we will be learning this poem about Arctic animals. Please read the poem with your child to help him or her learn it. Using the poem as a springboard, we will work with short vowel sounds, learn the *–ing* ending, and identify different short vowel sounds in a group of words (phoneme categorization) throughout the week.

Please assist your child in finding objects in the house that contain each of the five short vowel sounds listed in the attached Homework Book. After the objects have been located, have your child draw a picture of each object on the appropriate page and then write the word (or dictate it to you) on the line at the bottom of the page. Have your child bring the completed Homework Book to school on _____.

Your child will be bringing home an *Imagine* . . . Mini Book of the poem this week. Please ask him or her to read it to you. Your child may also want to read it to a special friend or relative.

Thank you for helpING!

Sincerely,

_____

Homework Book

My Short Vowel Sounds
Homework Book

By: _____

Aa    apple

1

_____

Homework Book

Ee  egg

_____ **2**

Ii  insect

_____ **3**

Homework Book

Oo octopus

4

_____

Uu umbrella

5

_____

Imagine . . . .

Hare

getting

Arctic

Jan

tan.

Nell

her

a

Lemming

ringing

Kip

sitting

an

bell.

Caribou

in

Freddy

Fox

warm

igloo.

the

wearing

Pete

eating

muffin.

socks.

Puffin

a

10

9

Imagine . . .

Arctic Hare Jan

getting a tan.

Lemming Nell

ringing her bell.

Kip Caribou

sitting in an igloo.

Freddy the Fox

wearing warm socks.

Pete Puffin

eating a muffin.

My favorite Arctic animal is _____

Imagine . . .

By: _____

Arctic Hare Jan

getting a tan.

2

Lemming Nell

3

ringing her bell.

Kip Caribou

sitting in an igloo.

Freddy the Fox

wearing warm socks.

 8

Pete Puffin

q

eating a muffin.

jumping

Circle all of the words ending in "ing."

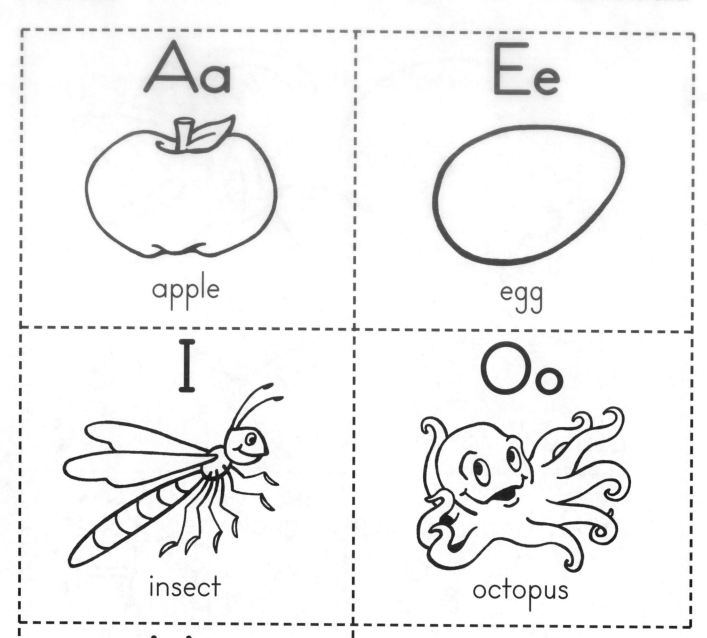

Aa
apple

Ee
egg

I
insect

Oo
octopus

Uu
umbrella

Animals in Winter

1, 2, birds fly, shoo!

3, 4, groundhogs start to snore.

5, 6, beavers gather sticks.

7, 8, bats in caves sleep late.

9, 10, bears snooze in their den.

1, 2, 3, 4, 5, 6, 7, 8, 9, 10!

Animals in Winter

Unit Preparation

Copy and send home the Animals in Winter Home/School Connection Parent Letter and Homework Page (pages 52–53). Copy and cut apart the Animals in Winter Pocket Chart Cards (pages 54–61). Copy, color, and cut apart the Animals in Winter Picture Cards (pages 62–64). Place all the cards in the pocket chart in the correct places. Copy the Animals in Winter Student Poem Page (page 65) and *Animals in Winter* Mini Book (pages 66–69) for each child. See page 4 for additional preparation suggestions.

Student Poem Page

Talk about animals in winter with the children. What animals have they seen during the winter? With the children's input, make a list of winter animals on the board or a chart. Briefly discuss where other animals go during the winter (e.g., hibernation, migration). Give each child a copy of the Animals in Winter Student Poem Page. Ask each child to choose his or her favorite winter animal. The child may choose one from the poem or another animal he or she knows. Guide the child to write the animal's name and something it does in winter on the blank lines at the bottom of the page. If the child is unable to write, he or she can dictate the words to you. Have the child draw a picture to illustrate the sentence.

Mini Book

Assemble an *Animals in Winter* Mini Book (pages 66–69) for each child. Have the children color the Mini Book pages and read it to a friend. At the end of the week, invite each child to take the book home and read it to his or her family.

Literature Links

Animals in Winter by Henrietta Bancroft (HarperTrophy, 1997)

Footprints in the Snow by Cynthia Benjamin (Cartwheel, 1994)

Sleepy Bear by Lydia Dabcovich (Puffin Books, 1985)

Time to Sleep by Denise Fleming (Henry Holt and Co., 2001)

What Will I Do Without You? by Sally Grindley (Kingfisher, 1999)

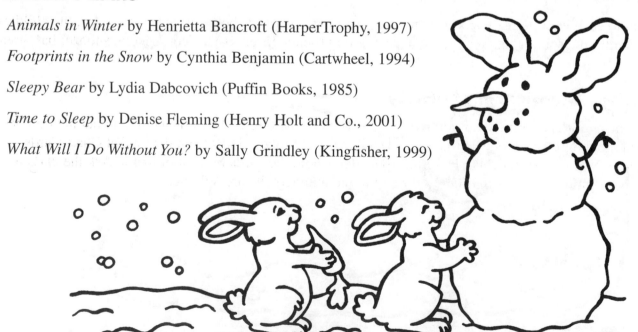

Pocket Chart Activities

Monday: Introduce the Poem

Read the poem, "Animals in Winter," aloud to the children. Reread the poem, pointing to the words in the chart as you go. Invite the children to read the poem aloud with you. How many animals are mentioned in the poem? Count them as a class.

Tuesday: Count Me In

After the children are familiar with the poem, remove the numbers from each line. Hand out number cards (see pages 60–61) to 10 students. Read the poem together, stopping at the spaces where the numbers belong. Ask the child holding the number needed to fill in the blank to place the number card in the correct place on the pocket chart. Continue reading the poem until all of the numbers have been replaced and then reread the poem together. You may wish to repeat this activity to give each student a turn.

Wednesday: Sneaky S's

Write the letter **s** on the board or chart paper. Review the sound that the letter makes. Ask the children to help you find the words in the poem that begin with the letter **s**. Read the poem together, then ask the children to raise their hand when they can find a word beginning with the letter **s**. Have a child remove the card from the poem and read the word beginning with the letter **s**. He or she may then return to his or her seat, taking the word. After all of the "s" words have been found, reread the poem, stopping where each blank is, and have the child with the correct word replace it in the poem. After all of the words have been replaced, have one student read the poem to the class.

Thursday: Phoneme Identity

Point to each word in the poem as you read each group of words below to your class. Ask the children to identify the sound that is the same in each group (**b**ears, **b**irds, **b**ats; **s**leeps, **s**nore, **s**nooze; ba**t**, grea**t**, bu**t**).

Friday: Culminating Activity

Ask the children to bring their completed homework to the circle. Have the children read the numbers aloud, pointing to each one as it is read. Hand out the numbers 1–10 from the Pocket Chart Cards (pages 60–61) to 10 students. Have the 10 students hold the cards in front of them. Ask the class to help you put the children in order according to the numbers the are holding.

Animals in Winter

1, 2, birds fly, shoo!

3, 4, groundhogs start to snore.

5, 6, beavers gather sticks.

7, 8, bats in caves sleep late.

9, 10, bears snooze in their den.

1, 2, 3, 4, 5, 6, 7, 8, 9, 10!

Hello,

This week we will be learning this poem about animals in winter. Please read the poem with your child to help him or her learn it. Using the poem as a springboard, we will work on counting to 10, identifying the same sound in different words (phoneme identity), and finding the words beginning with the letter **s** throughout the week.

Please help your child cut out the number cards on the Homework Page. First, have your child count the number of animals on each card. Then, arrange the cards in numerical order. Paste them in the correct order on a separate sheet of paper. Please send the completed page to school on _____.

Your child will be bringing home an *Animals in Winter* Mini Book of the poem this week. Please ask him or her to read it to you. Your child may also want to read it to a special friend or relative.

Thank you for your participation. I knew I could "count" on you!

Sincerely,

_____

Homework Page

Directions: Cut out the number cards below. Count the number of animals on each card. Arrange the cards in numerical order. Paste the cards in the correct order on a separate sheet of paper.

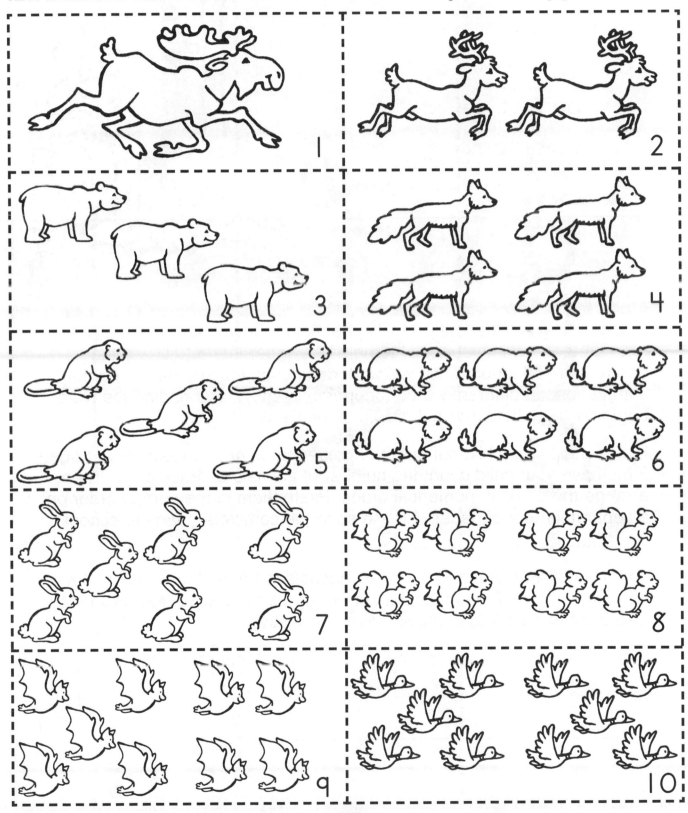

Animals

in Winter

2,

fly,

3,

1,

birds

shoo!

groundhogs

start

4,

snore.

to

6,

gather

7,

5,

beavers

sticks.

bats

caves

late.

&,

in

sleep

10,

snooze

their

9,

bears

in

1,

3,

5,

den.

2,

4,

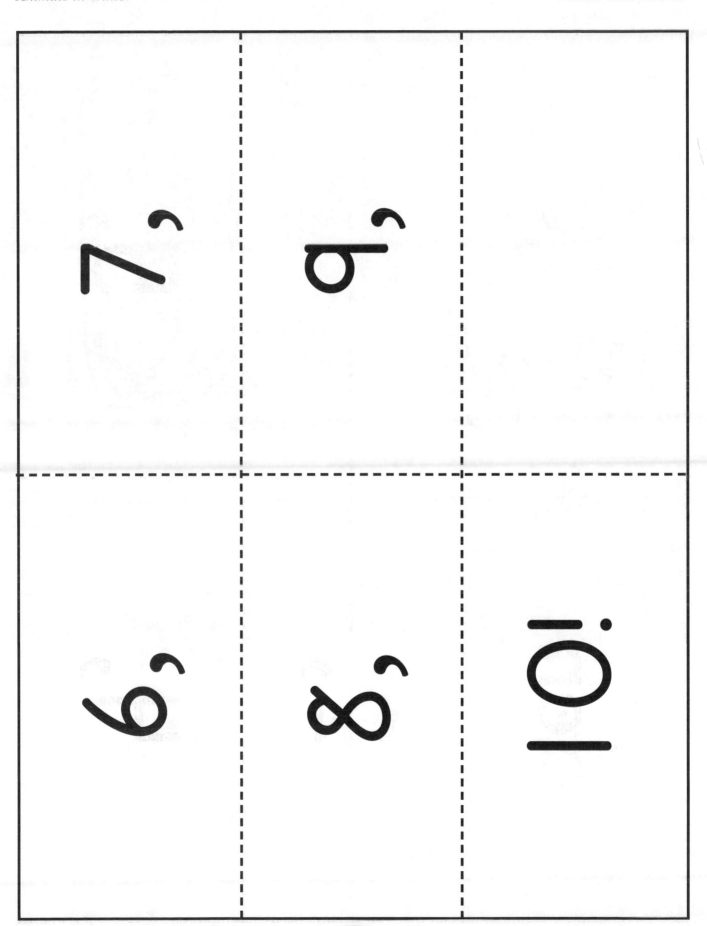

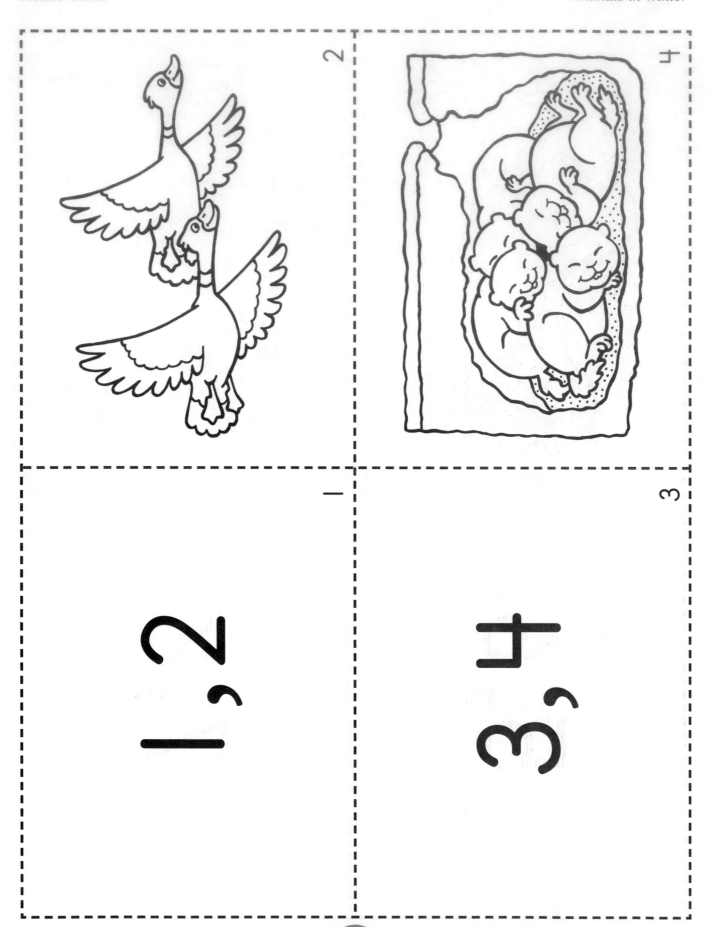

2

4

1

3

1, 2

3, 4

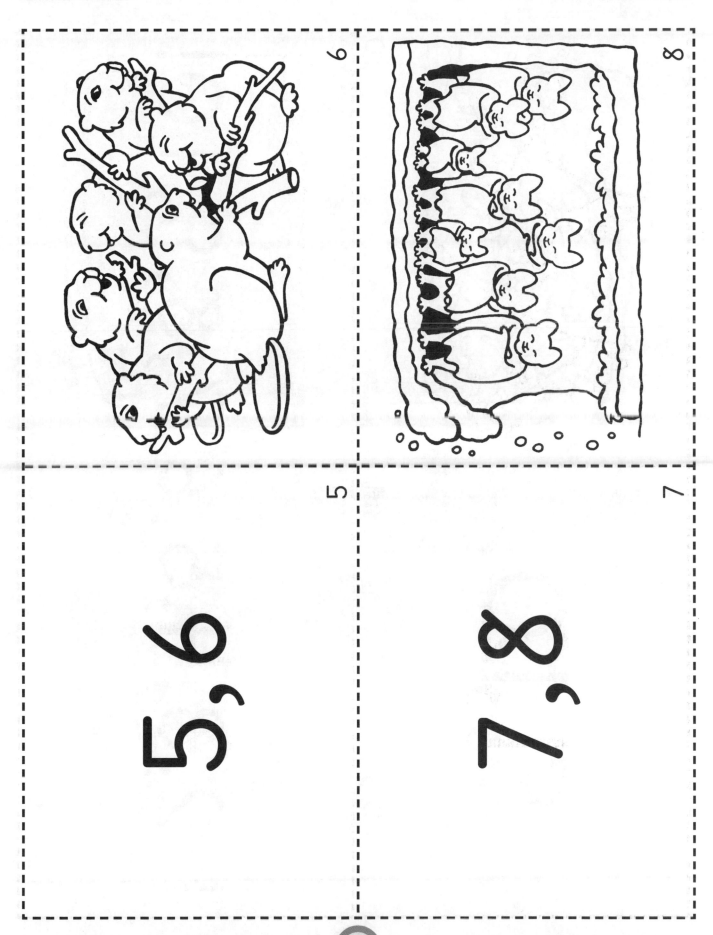

6

8

5

7

5, 6

7, 8

10

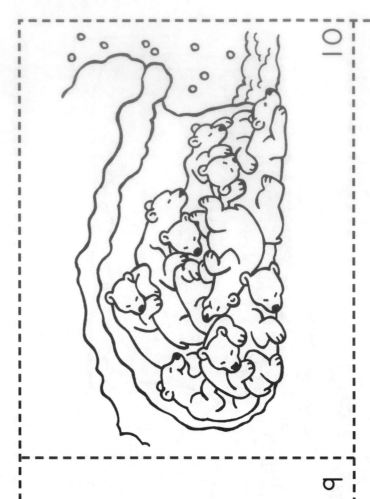

9

9, 10

11

1, 2, 3, 4, 5, 6, 7, 8, 9, 10!

Animals in Winter

1, 2, birds fly, shoo!

3, 4, groundhogs start to snore.

5, 6, beavers gather sticks.

7, 8, bats in caves sleep late.

9, 10, bears snooze in their den.

1, 2, 3, 4, 5, 6, 7, 8, 9, 10!

A _____ _____ in winter.
 (animal)   (does what?)

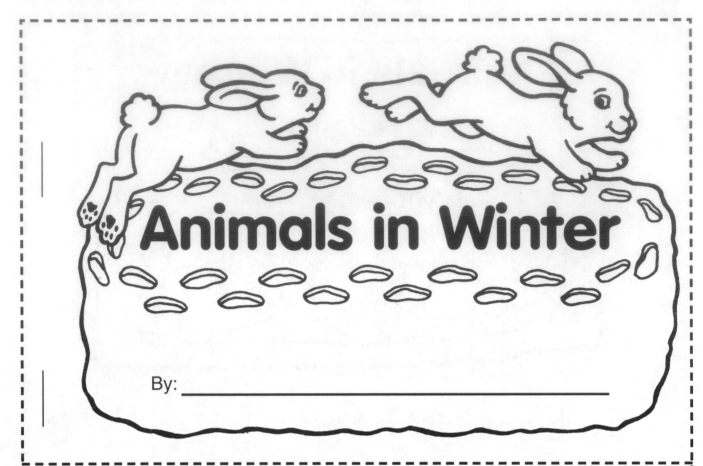

Animals in Winter

By: _____

1, 2, birds fly, shoo!

1

3, 4, groundhogs start to snore. **2**

5,6, beavers gather sticks. **3**

#3141 A Poem In My Pocket: Winter

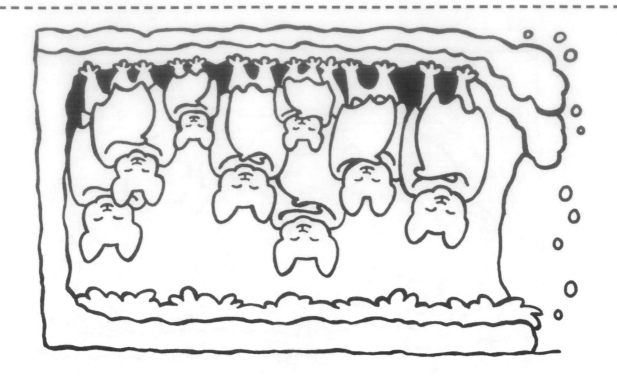

7, 8, bats in caves sleep late. 4

9, 10, bears snooze in their den. 5

1, 2, 3, 4, 5, 6, 7, 8, 9, 10!   **6**

Find all the commas in the book and circle them. Remember to pause in your reading when you see a comma.   **7**

Planets

Mercury and Venus,

Earth and then Mars,

Jupiter and Saturn

Are planets, not stars.

Uranus and Neptune,

Some are large, some are small.

Look for tiny Pluto.

Can you name them all?

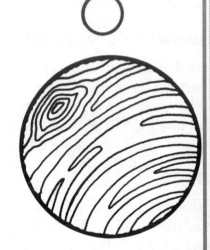

Planets

Unit Preparation

Copy and send home the Planets Home/School Connection Parent Letter and Homework Page (pages 73–74). Copy and cut apart the Planets Pocket Chart Cards (pages 75–80). Copy, color, and cut out the Planets Picture Cards (pages 81–82). Place all the cards in the pocket chart in the correct places. Copy, color, and cut out the Planets Map (page 89). Copy and cut out the Planets Number Cards (page 90). Write each of your students' names on a 3" x 5" card or pocket chart card for Tuesday's activity. Copy the Planets Student Poem Page (page 83) and *Planets* Mini Book pages (pages 84–88) for each child. See page 4 for additional preparation tips.

Student Poem Page

Ask the children what they know about the nine planets. Make a list of the planets on the board or a chart and list a fact about each planet. Ask the children to think about which planet they would like to visit. On the blank at the bottom of the Student Poem Page, assist each child in writing the name of that planet. Ask each child to draw a picture of that planet in the space provided. Refer to the illustration on page 70 as necessary.

Mini Book

Assemble a *Planets* Mini Book (pages 84–88) for each child. Have the children color the pages and read their Mini Books to others. At the end of the week, invite each child to take the book home and read it to his or her family.

Literature Links

Company's Coming by Arthur Yorinks (Hyperion, 2000)

The Planets by Gail Gibbons (Holiday House, 2005)

The Planets in Our Solar System by Franklyn M. Branley (HarperTrophy, 1998)

The Soccer Mom from Outer Space by Barney Saltzberg (Crown Books for Young Readers, 2000)

Twinkle, Twinkle, Little Star by Iza Trapani (Charlesbridge Publishing, Board edition, 1998)

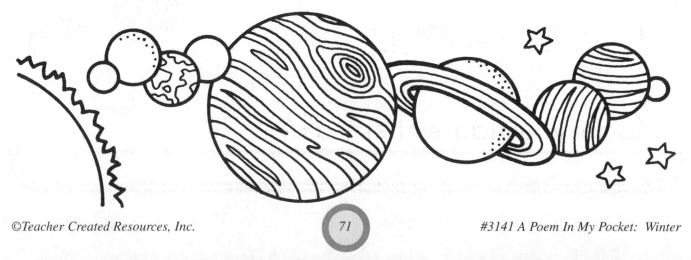

Pocket Chart Activities

Monday: Introduce the Poem

Read the poem, "Planets," aloud to the children. Reread the poem, pointing to the words as you go. Invite the children to read the poem aloud with you. Hold up the Planets Map (page 89) for the class to see. Name each planet as you point to it.

Tuesday: Clap and Count

Remove the poem from the pocket chart and place the Number Cards (page 90) in the pocket chart as shown in the illustration. Give each child the name card you have prepared for him or her (see page 71, Unit Preparation). Tell the class that you are going to learn about syllables, or the number of parts a word has. Tell the children that each one of their names contains a certain number of syllables and you are going to figure out how many syllables are in each child's name. Demonstrate saying your name and clapping for each syllable. Next demonstrate an incorrect breakdown of syllables (for example, *Be-en*, two syllables for Ben instead of the correct one syllable). Give each child a chance to clap and count the syllables in his or her name, giving assistance as needed. After each child has correctly determined how many syllables are in his or her name, have the child place the name card under the correct number in the pocket chart. The children will need repeated practice to understand this concept. Place the poem back in the pocket chart after this activity.

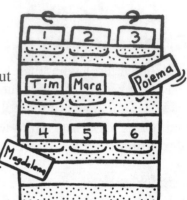

Wednesday: Phoneme Deletion

In Phoneme Deletion, children are able to recognize that a new word remains when phonemes are removed from a word.

> **Teacher:** What is *slip* without the /s/ sound?
>
> **Students:** *Slip* without the /s/ sound is *lip*.

Practice phoneme deletion using the following words from the poem: *small, /s/; for, /f/; can, /c/*. After the class has told you the new word, remove the word from the poem and cover up the first letter to check their answer for accuracy.

Thursday: Planets Sort

Remove all of the cards from the pocket chart, setting the planet name cards aside. Put the Planets Number Cards (page 90) in the pocket chart as in Tuesday's activity, using only number cards 1–4. Spread out the planet name cards (Pocket Chart Cards, pages 75–80) on the floor and have a volunteer choose a card, clap and count the syllables, and place the card under the correct number card in the pocket chart. Place the poem back in the pocket chart after this activity.

Friday: Culminating Activity

Invite the children to bring their Homework Pages to the circle. Go through the number of syllables, giving each child an opportunity to share what he or she found by saying and clapping the word. Reread the poem together to conclude the unit.

Planets

Mercury and Venus,
Earth and then Mars,
Jupiter and Saturn
Are planets, not stars.
Uranus and Neptune,
Some are large, some are small.
Look for tiny Pluto.
Can you name them all?

Hello,

This week we will be learning this poem about planets. Please read the poem with your child to help him or her learn it. Using the poem as a springboard, we will work on counting syllables and removing one sound from a word to make a new word (phoneme deletion). For example, *slip* without the /s/ sound is *lip*.

Please help your child complete the Homework Page by helping him or her find objects around the house that have one, two, three, or four syllables in their name. After you have located the objects, have your child draw and write the name of each object in the correct box. (You can write it for him or her if needed.) Please send the completed homework to school on _____.

Your child will be bringing home a *Planets* Mini Book of the poem this week. Please ask him or her to read it to you. Your child may also want to read it to a special friend or relative.

I know I can "count" on you to make this activity a success!

Sincerely,

_____

Homework Page

Directions: Find objects around the house that have one, two, three, or four syllables in their names. Draw a picture and write the name of each object in the correct box.

1 syllable as in *Earth*	2 syllables as in *Venus*
3 syllables as in *Mercury*	4 syllables as in *binoculars*

Planets

Mercury and

Venus,

and

Mars,

and

Earth

then

Jupiter

Are

not

Uranus

Saturn

planets,

stars.

Neptune,

are

some

and

Some

large,

small.

for

Pluto.

are

Look

tiny

you

them

Can

name

all?

Planets

Mercury and Venus,
Earth and then Mars,
Jupiter and Saturn
Are planets, not stars.

Uranus and Neptune,
Some are large, some are small.
Look for tiny Pluto.
Can you name them all?

I would like to visit _____

Planets

By: _____

Mercury and Venus,

1

84

Earth and then Mars,

2

Jupiter and Saturn

3

#3141 A Poem In My Pocket: Winter

Are planets, not stars.

4

Uranus and Neptune,

5

86

Some are large, some are small.

Look for tiny Pluto.

Can you name them all?   **8**

Earth

Underline each planet named in
the book.   **9**

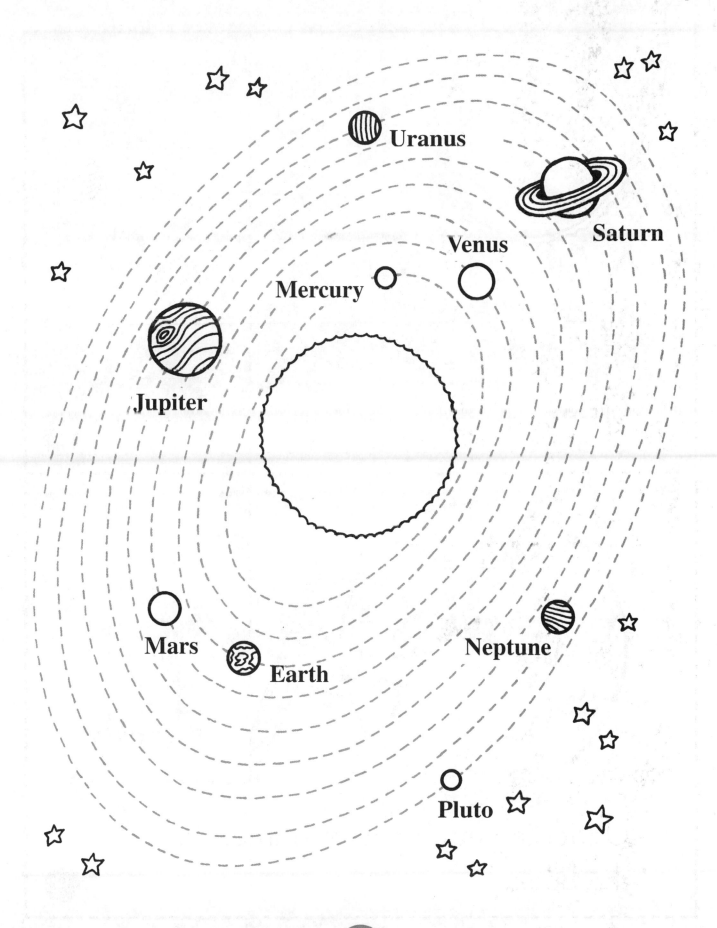

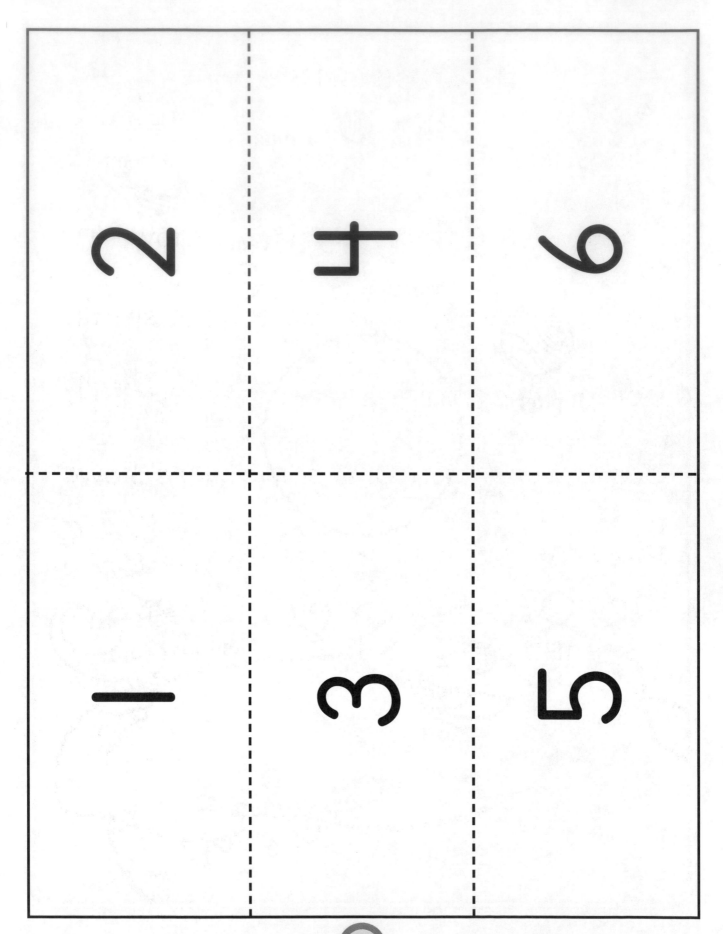

Dinosaurs

Dinosaurs lived long ago.

They were different, this we know.

Some were big, and some were small.

Some were short, and some were tall.

Some were fast, and some were slow.

How many kinds do you know?

Dinosaurs

Unit Preparation

Copy and send home the Dinosaurs Home/School Connection Parent Letter and Homework Page
(pages 94–95). Copy and cut apart the Dinosaurs Pocket Chart Cards (pages 96–102). Copy, color, and
cut out the Dinosaurs Picture Cards (pages 103–104). Place all the cards in the pocket chart in the
correct places. Copy and cut apart the Dinosaurs Rhyming Cards (pages 111–112). Copy and color the
Dinosaur Page (page 110). Enlarge this page if possible. Copy the Dinosaurs Student Poem Page
(page 105) and *Dinosaurs* Mini Book pages (pages 106–109) for each child. See page 4 for additional
preparation tips.

Student Poem Page

Ask children to tell how dinosaurs were alike. Then ask them how they were different. Focus on
characteristics such as size, eating habits, and how they moved. After the children are familiar with the
poem, ask them to think about which kind of dinosaur they might like the best (big, small, short, tall,
fast, or slow). Then have them copy the corresponding word from the poem onto the blank at the
bottom of their Student Poem Pages (page 105). Allow the children time to illustrate their poems in the
space provided.

Mini Books

Assemble a *Dinosaurs* Mini Book for each child. Have the children color the pages and read their Mini
Books to others. At the end of the week, invite each child to take the book home and read it to his or
her family.

Literature Links

Bones, Bones, Dinosaur Bones by Byron Barton (HarperCollins, 1990)

Dinosaur Roar! by Paul Stickland (Dutton Books, 1997)

How Do Dinosaurs Say Goodnight? by Jane Yolen (Blue Sky Press, 2000)

Oh My Oh My Oh Dinosaurs! by Sandra Boynton (Workman Publishing, 1993)

Whatever Happened to the Dinosaurs? by Bernard Most (Voyager Books, 1987)

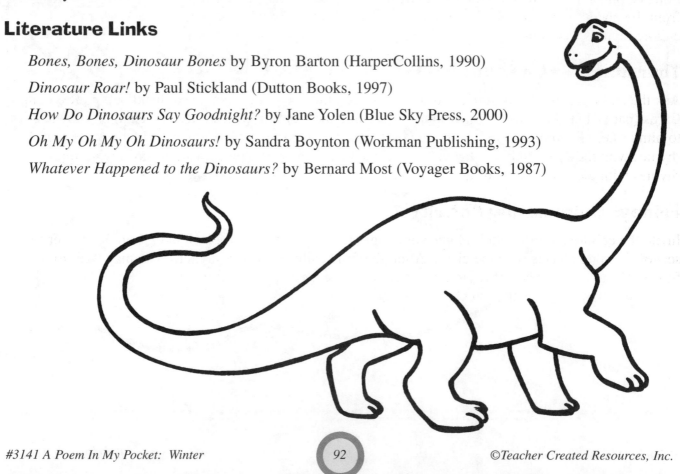

Pocket Chart Activities

Monday: Introduce the Poem

Read the poem, "Dinosaurs," aloud to the children. Reread the poem, pointing to the words as you go. Invite the children to read the poem aloud with you. Ask the children if they know the names of any dinosaurs. Hold up the Dinosaur Page (page 110) for the class to see. (Enlarge the page if possible.) Have the children help you identify each of the dinosaurs on the page by name. Ask the children to help you find the big, small, short, and tall dinosaurs.

Tuesday: Rhyme Time

Ask the children to tell you what rhyming words are. Explain that rhyming words have the same sound at the end. Give the children a few examples of rhyming word pairs. Ask the children if they think there are any rhyming words in the poem. Read the poem together, asking the children to listen for rhyming words, but not to say anything aloud. When you have finished reading the poem, ask volunteers to find rhyming pairs in the poem's text. Have the class determine if the pairs that are found are actually rhyming words. After all of the pairs have been identified, reread the poem together.

Wednesday: Phoneme Segmentation

In Phoneme Segmentation, children break a word into separate sounds.

    Teacher: How many sounds are in *chip*?

    Students: /ch/ /i/ /p/. There are three sounds in *chip*.

Practice phoneme segmentation with your class as in the example above using the following words from the poem: *big, tall, fast, know, small.* Point to each word in the text of the poem after the children have successfully broken it down.

Thursday: Find a Rhyme

Ask the class to listen for rhyming words as you read the poem together. Next, hand out the Rhyming Cards (pages 111–112) to several volunteers, reading the word on the card to each child as you hand it to him or her. Read the poem together and ask each volunteer to listen for a word in the poem that rhymes with the word on his or her card. Ask each child that is holding a card to say a word that rhymes with the word on his or her card. Have the class help as needed.

Friday: Culminating Activity

Invite the children to bring their Homework Pages to the circle. Ask each child to share his or her two sets of rhyming objects with the class. After all of the children have had a turn, you may want to further expand on each set of rhyming words by asking the class if they can think of any other words that rhyme with the objects each child picked. Reread the poem together one final time.

Dinosaurs

Dinosaurs lived long ago.

They were different, this we know.

Some were big, and some were small.

Some were short, and some were tall.

Some were fast, and some were slow.

How many kinds do you know?

Hello,

This week we will be learning this poem about dinosaurs. Please read the poem with your child to help him or her learn it. Using the poem as a springboard, we will be working with identifying and creating rhymes, and breaking words into individual sounds to create words (phoneme segmentation) throughout the week.

Please help your child find two pairs of objects that rhyme. If you are unable to find rhyming objects in your home, your child may draw pictures of objects from memory. Draw the rhyming pairs on the Homework Page and assist your child in filling in the blanks, or write the words for him or her. Send the homework to school on _____.

Your child will be bringing home a *Dinosaurs* Mini Book of the poem this week. Please ask him or her to read it to you. He or she may also want to read it to a special friend or relative.

Thank YOU for what you DO!

Sincerely,

_____

Homewok Page

Directions: Find two pairs of objects that rhyme. Draw the rhyming pairs. Write the word for each object on the appropriate blank.

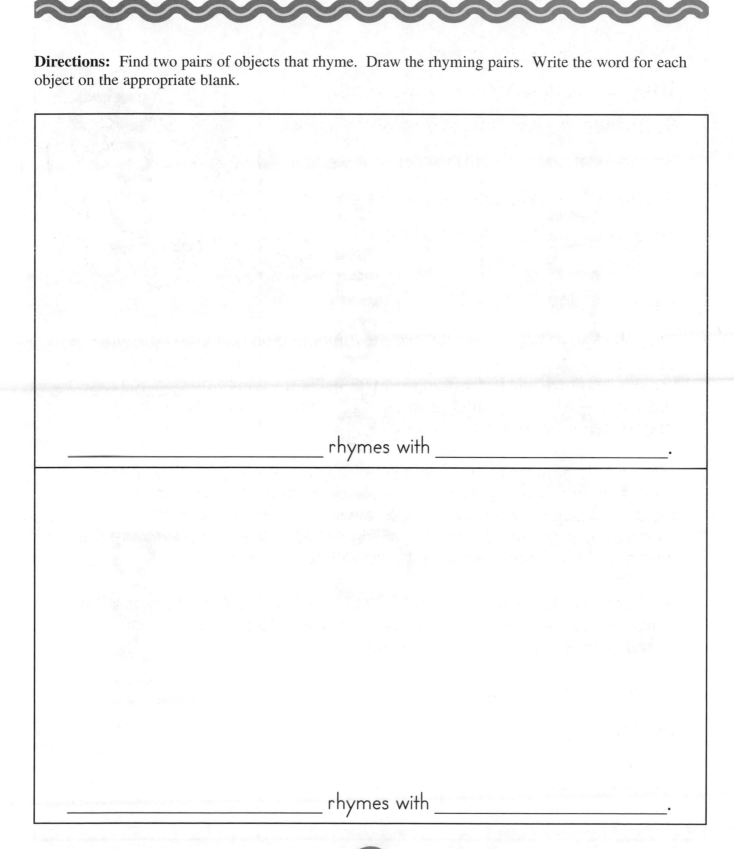

_____ rhymes with _____.

_____ rhymes with _____.

Dinosaurs

Dinosaurs

long

lived

They

this

different,

ago.

were

know.

were

and

we

Some

big,

were

Some

short,

some

small.

were

some

tall.

were

and

were

Some

and

were

How

fast,

some

slow.

kinds

you

many

do

know?

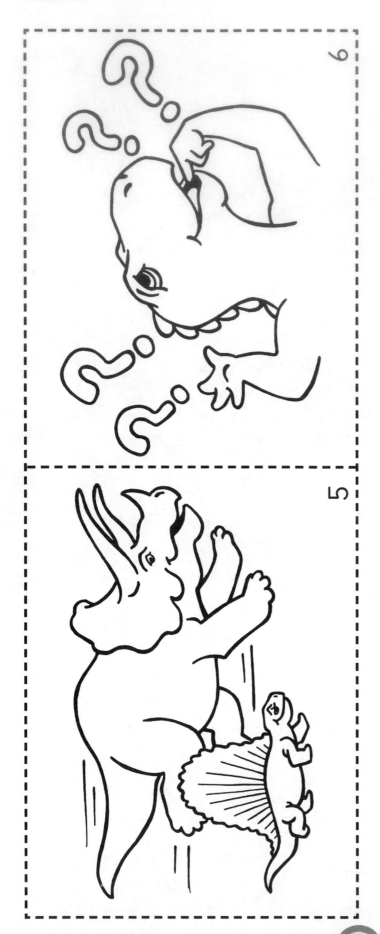

6

5

Dinosaurs

Dinosaurs lived long ago.

They were different, this we know.

Some were big, and some were small.

Some were short, and some were tall.

Some were fast, and some were slow.

How many kinds do you know?

I like _____dinosaurs the best.

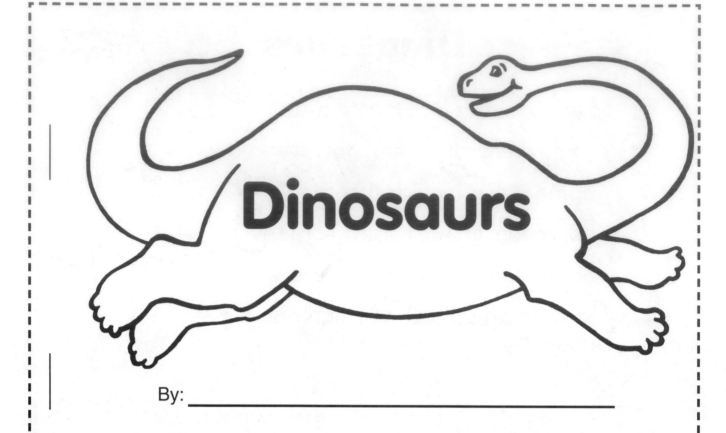

By: _____

Dinosaurs lived long ago.

They were different, this we know.

Some were big, and some were small. **3**

Some were short, and some were tall.

Some were fast, and some were slow. **5**

How many kinds do you know?

cat   bat

Find two words that rhyme and underline them with the same color.

Continue until you have underlined all the rhyming pairs.

7

Parasaurolophus

Pteranodon

Brachiosaurus

Triceratops

Dimetrodon

Tylosaurus

Tyrannosaurus

Ankylosaurus

Stegosaurus

Oviraptor

Use the cards below and on page 112 for the Find a Rhyme Activity described on page 93 (Thursday).

ball

pig

snow

bow

Use the cards below and on page 111 for the Rhyming Activity described on page 93.

hay

tree

glue

cast